TAKE TEN YEARS

1950s

Published by Evans Brothers Limited
2A Portman Mansions
Chiltern Street
London W1U 6NR

Typeset by Fleetlines Typesetters, Southend-on-Sea
Printed in Spain by GRAFO, S.A. - Bilbao

ISBN 0 237 51664 0

Acknowledgements

Maps – Jillian Luff of Bitmap Graphics
Design – Neil Sayer
Editor – Caroline Sheldrick

For permission to reproduce copyright material the author and
publishers gratefully acknowledge the following:

Cover photographs – (Hillary and Tenzing) Topham, (all others)
Popperfoto
Page 4 – The Hulton Picture Company, Popperfoto, Topham,
AllSport, Associated Press/Topham; page 5 – Popperfoto, Science
Photo Library, Popperfoto, Topham, The Vintage Magazine
Company; page 8 – Topham; page 9 – Popperfoto; page 10 – (top)
The Vintage Magazine Company, (bottom left, right) Popperfoto;
page 11 – The Hulton Picture Company; page 12 – (left) Popperfoto,
(right) Popperfoto; page 13 – (top left, top right, bottom)
Popperfoto; page 14 – Topham; page 15 – (top, bottom) Popperfoto;
page 16 – Popperfoto; page 17 – (top) Popperfoto, (bottom) Agence
Nature/NHPA; page 18 – Topham; page 19 – (left) The Vintage
Magazine Company (right) Popperfoto; page 20 – (top, bottom)
Popperfoto; page 21 – Popperfoto; page 23 – (left, right)
Popperfoto; page 24 – Popperfoto; page 26 – (left, right)
Popperfoto; page 27 (top left and right) The Hulton Picture
Company, (bottom) Popperfoto; page 29 – (top, bottom)
Popperfoto; page 30 – (left, right) Popperfoto; page 31 – (top,
middle) Popperfoto, (bottom) Topham; page 32 – Popperfoto; page
33 – (top left, right) Popperfoto, (bottom) Science Photo Library;
page 34 – (left) Popperfoto, (right) The Vintage Magazine
Company; page 35 – Popperfoto; page 36 – (left, right) Popperfoto;
page 37 – (left) The Vintage Magazine Company, (right) Photofest/
Retna Pictures Ltd; page 38 – (top, bottom) Popperfoto; page 39 –
Popperfoto; page 40 – Popperfoto; page 41 – (top, bottom)
Popperfoto; page 42 – (left) Popperfoto, (right) The Vintage
Magazine Company; page 43 – (left) Topham, (right) Popperfoto;
page 44 – (1, 2) The Vintage Magazine Company, (3, 4, 5) The
Advertising Archives; page 45 – (1, 2) The Vintage Magazine
Company, (3) © 1959, General Motors Corporation. Reproduced
with permission of General Motors Corporation/Advertising
Archives, (4) The Advertising Archives, (5) The Vintage Magazine
Company, (6) The Advertising Archives.

TAKE TEN YEARS

1950s

MARGARET SHARMAN

EVANS BROTHERS LIMITED

Contents

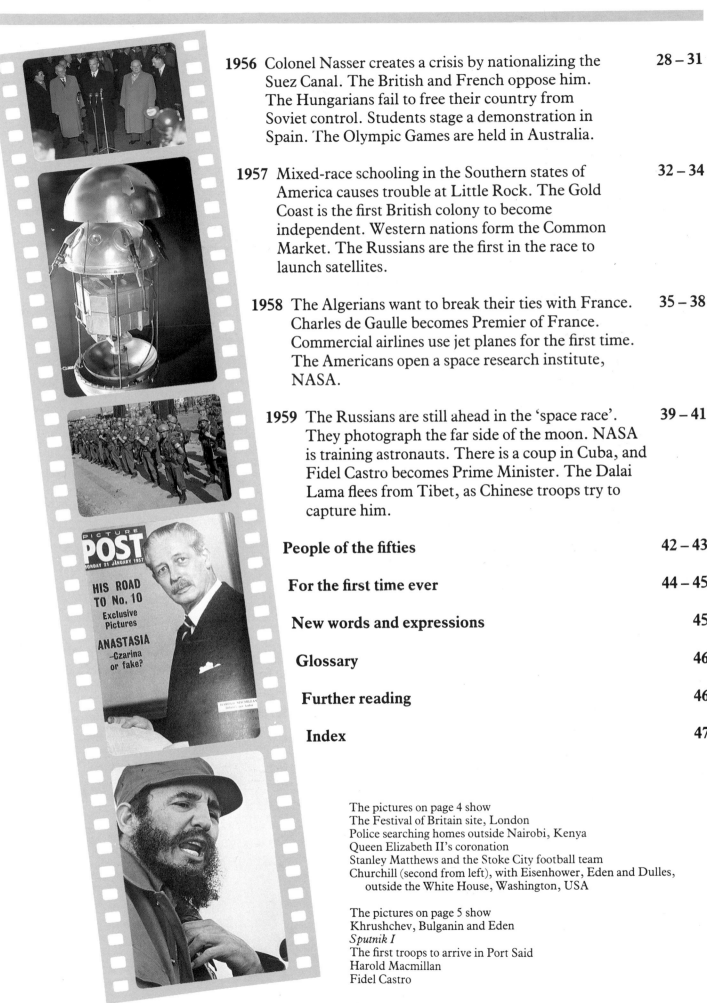

The pictures on page 4 show
The Festival of Britain site, London
Police searching homes outside Nairobi, Kenya
Queen Elizabeth II's coronation
Stanley Matthews and the Stoke City football team
Churchill (second from left), with Eisenhower, Eden and Dulles, outside the White House, Washington, USA

The pictures on page 5 show
Khrushchev, Bulganin and Eden
Sputnik I
The first troops to arrive in Port Said
Harold Macmillan
Fidel Castro

Introduction

In 1950, the effects of World War II were still present. Major European cities had been badly bombed, and new houses, factories and shops had to be built. Food was still in short supply and rationing continued in Britain up until the mid-fifties.

There was much unrest in countries occupied by foreign rulers. In Africa, the British granted independence to the Gold Coast, and it became Ghana. Kenyans struggled for freedom and more land in a guerrilla war known as the Mau Mau rebellion. The Egyptians seized the Suez Canal, which the British and French had controlled for 75 years. The French had to leave Vietnam, and also faced guerrilla fighters in Algeria. The Tibetans resisted the Chinese, and the Hungarians tried to rid themselves of the Russians.

Many of these conflicts could have led to a third world war, as the superpowers took opposite sides. The dreadful threat of nuclear weapons may have averted war. Also, the United Nations was able to defuse some dangerous conflicts. But between East and West, the deadly Cold War continued. Towards the end of the decade this Cold War had thawed a little, but several smaller countries were still danger spots.

It was also a decade when mankind reached out for new knowledge. Nuclear power stations began to create electricity, but at the same time H-bombs were tested. People were nervous about the threat of nuclear war. Nobody wanted that. They were encouraged by the spectacular achievements in a new direction: the Russians launched the world's first artificial satellite, and the Americans trained astronauts for space flight. It seemed as if science fiction was coming true.

YEARS	WORLD AFFAIRS
1950	US and USSR are rivals; the US is afraid of Communist power in the East
1951	The Cold War: trials of suspected spies Baudouin becomes King of the Belgians
1952	Coup in Egypt Hussein becomes King of Jordan King George VI is succeeded by Queen Elizabeth II
1953	Queen crowned; she tours the Commonwealth Power struggle in USSR when Stalin dies
1954	Nasser leads Egyptian Republic SEATO formed Events in Vietnam may have a domino effect
1955	Warsaw Pact signed S. Vietnam becomes a Republic
1956	Nasser takes over Suez Canal Cold War begins to thaw
1957	Gold Coast becomes Ghana Common Market formed Russians launch Sputniks
1958	General de Gaulle is Premier of France Egypt and Syria become UAR King Feisal of Iraq murdered
1959	Castro takes over in Cuba The space race is on Dalai Lama flees from Tibet

WARS & REVOLTS	PEOPLE	EVENTS
The North Koreans invade South Korea	McCarthy accuses people of being Communists Frank Sinatra sings in London	The Stone of Scone is stolen Holy Year celebrated at the Vatican *Eagle* comic is launched
North Koreans pushed back	Maclean and Burgess disappear from British Foreign Office Churchill becomes Prime Minister again	The Festival of Britain
Mau Mau uprising in Kenya	Dr. Linse abducted in Berlin Agatha Christie's *Mousetrap* opens	Olympic Games in Finland Americans test H-bomb Coelacanth discovered
East German revolt	Hillary and Tenzing climb Everest Watson and Crick discover DNA Dr. Salk's polio vaccine	The Stanley Matthews Cup Final
French fight N. Vietnamese	Roger Bannister runs mile in 4 minutes Oppenheimer not allowed to see atomic secrets	Food rationing ends in Britain Rabbits killed by myxomatosis
Civil war in Cyprus	Martin Luther King leads fight against prejudice James Dean is killed	Bus boycott in Alabama First advertisements on TV in Britain
Hungarians revolt against Russian rule Conflict over Suez Spanish demonstrations against Franco	Khrushchev in England Grace Kelly becomes a Princess Archbishop Makarios exiled	Olympic Games in Australia *Under Milk Wood* performed Britain's first power station opened
	Beatniks in USA and England Macmillan becomes Prime Minister of Britain	Little Rock School admits black pupils
Civil war in Algeria	Pope John XXIII crowned Elvis Presley joins army Pasternak wins Nobel Prize	NASA opened in USA Jet service to USA begins Plane crash kills soccer players First Aldermaston march
Coup in Cuba More trouble in S. Vietnam	Khrushchev visits America Charles van Doren wins quizzes by fraud Makarios is President of Cyprus	Russians photograph other side of the moon Britain's first motorway

1950

THE WAR IN KOREA

NORTH KOREANS INVADE SOUTH

June 25, The Far East Korea is divided into two countries. North Korea is a Communist republic. South Korea is a democratic republic. The boundary between the two is the line of latitude 38°, known as the 38th parallel.

Today 60,000 North Korean soldiers, with Russian tanks and jet planes, crossed the 38th parallel, and invaded South Korea. The invasion has alarmed the Western powers. The United States helped South Korea after World War II. The USSR and the United States seem to be taking opposite sides in this dispute.

UNITED NATIONS STEPS IN

June 30, South Korea The North Korean army has captured South Korea's capital, Seoul. The South Koreans do not have a proper army, and their weapons are out of date. The United Nations has asked its members to help South Korea. The first American troops arrived today.

GENERAL MACARTHUR TAKES COMMAND

July 7, South Korea General MacArthur of the United States is commander of all forces in South Korea. Jet planes are bombing Pyongyang, the Northern capital. But the strong North Korean forces are resisting the UN army.

AMERICANS FORCED BACK TO PUSAN

Sept 1, South Korea The UN forces have been pushed right back to Pusan, on the south-east coast. Today they were joined by British troops. Their enemies, the North Koreans, began a terrific bombardment today along an 80-km (50-mile) front. The war is not going well for the UN forces.

UN troops in action in Korea

A SECOND FRONT IS OPENED

Sept 15, South Korea Over 250 ships have arrived at Inchon, on the west coast. They are troop carriers bringing in US soldiers. The country around Inchon is held by their enemies, the North Koreans. The US soldiers will fight their way towards Pusan. This will not be easy; the roads are mined and the opposition is very great. But it means that the enemy has to fight two armies.

UN FORCES ON THE OFFENSIVE

Oct 9, South Korea   The troops from Inchon managed to reach Pusan. The two armies fought their way north and recaptured Seoul. Today they crossed the 38th parallel.

There is now a new threat, this time from China. President Chou En-lai said the UN troops had no right to invade North Korea.

UN FORCES HAVE TO WITHDRAW

Oct 27, North Korea   At least 14 Chinese divisions have crossed into Korea. The UN forces are heavily outnumbered. Russian MiG planes are bombing their positions. They are retreating back towards the 38th parallel.

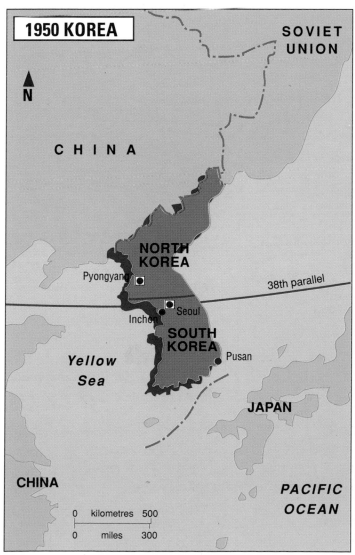

Korea is divided at the 38th parallel.

UN FORCES FACE DEFEAT

Dec 24, South Korea   The UN army has lost all the ground it gained. In spite of this disaster, President Truman will not allow the army to use atomic bombs. The troops are back at the American base at Pusan.

CROWDS RECEIVE POPE'S BLESSING

July 9, Vatican City   This is Holy Year for Roman Catholics. From all over the world pilgrims are coming to Rome. The Vatican staff have put up tents on the surrounding hills. One of the Fathers has been especially thoughtful to English visitors. He has arranged for a tea-room to be opened. He knows that to an English visitor a 'cuppa' is always welcome.

Today the Pope, Pius XII, blessed the huge crowd of pilgrims from an upper window of his residence in Vatican City.

His Holiness Pope Pius XII

SENATOR SEES REDS EVERYWHERE

Feb 20, Washington, USA A British nuclear scientist, Dr. Klaus Fuchs, has admitted that he supplied atomic secrets to the Russians. Suddenly Americans realize that the Russians may be making atomic bombs too. They are frightened of a nuclear war. Senator Joseph McCarthy is taking advantage of their fear. He accuses over 200 people in the State Department of being secret Communists. He gives no proof of this, but people believe him.

DISAPPEARANCE OF A STONE

Dec 29, Scotland The historic Stone of Scone is missing. This lump of sandstone sat under the Coronation chair in Westminster Abbey, London. It came from Scone in Scotland 650 years ago. An anonymous letter says the burglars will tell the police where it is, so long as the stone can stay in Scotland. The English are not likely to agree. Their kings and queens are crowned on the Stone of Scone. The police are searching for it in Scotland.

NEWS IN BRIEF . . .

HARRY LIME, MYSTERY MAN

Jan 13, London *The Third Man* opens in the West End today. It is a film about Harry Lime (played by Orson Welles), who is hunted through Vienna by his one-time friend. The hunt takes them through the sewers, and on a giant wheel at a fairground. The film has a haunting background tune, played on a zither.

SPACE IS AN EXCITING PLACE

April 14, London *Eagle*, a new strip cartoon weekly paper, is on sale for the first time today. On the front page Dan Dare and his fat friend Digby fight the forces of evil from other galaxies. Inside, Luck of the Legion fights with desert 'baddies', cowboys battle with Indians, and highwaymen lurk in the shadows. The drawings by Frank Hampson are superb. *Eagle* is on sale every Friday, price threepence.

The front page of the *Eagle*

NEAT AND SMART IS FASHIONABLE

Spring, London Nylon stockings are as popular as ever. They are held up with suspenders from the new elastic roll-on girdles. These are a perfect foundation for Dior's sheath dresses and tailored skirts. For dancing, wide skirts over several petticoats are set off by a wide belt. Blouses are soft nylon. Make-up is very important for eyes and lips. Nail varnish matches the lipstick.

Young men on the dance floor wear suits and ties. The Fifty-Shilling Tailor, with branches in every town, can supply a ready-to-wear suit for under £3. A girl likes her escort to look smart.

SINGER DELIGHTS HIS FANS

July 15, London Frank Sinatra is singing to packed audiences in London this week. He is the most popular singer in the United States. Bing Crosby once said, "He has the voice of a lifetime – but why did it have to happen in mine?"

1951

SPIES AND SUSPECTED SPIES
HISS'S APPEAL FAILS

March 12, New York Last year Alger Hiss, an American lawyer, denied in court that he spied for Russia. The court found Hiss not guilty, but said he had lied while under oath. He was sentenced to five years in prison. Hiss appealed, but today the appeal court has not reduced his sentence. People still wonder if he was in fact a spy.

FOREIGN OFFICE MEN DISAPPEAR

June 8, London Two senior Foreign Office officials, Donald Maclean and Guy Burgess, have been missing since Friday May 25. On the following Monday, officers from the British secret service were going to question Maclean. They suspected him of spying for the USSR. The government is wondering whether someone warned Maclean. Police are searching for them all over Europe.

POLICE QUESTION A THIRD MAN

Nov 30, London An inquiry has opened into the Burgess and Maclean affair. A diplomat named Kim Philby was recalled from his job at the British Embassy in Washington to answer questions. Guy Burgess stayed in Philby's house there. As a senior Foreign Office official, Philby knew Maclean was going to be questioned in May. The inquiry found nothing to suggest that he was guilty.

ROSENBERGS FOUND GUILTY

April 5, New York Julius and Ethel Rosenberg have been sentenced to death for spying for Russia. They are accused of obtaining information about the atomic bomb in 1944. David Greenglass, who worked on the bomb project, passed information to Rosenberg. He passed it on to an agent named Harry Gold. Greenglass and Gold confessed, but the Rosenbergs said they were innocent. The Rosenbergs are Communists. Their lawyer says they cannot get a fair trial because of Senator McCarthy's anti-Communist activities.

Ethel and Julius Rosenberg after their trial

THE GIs ARE COMING BACK

June 18, London The British government will allow the United States to build an air base in England. It will be at Greenham Common in Berkshire. The Americans will have fighter and bomber planes here permanently. The local householders are not happy with this decision.

FESTIVAL A TONIC TO THE NATION

June 1, London The Festival of Britain is raising our spirits with its colour and gaiety. All along the South Bank of the River Thames, mudflats have been drained and old houses pulled down. In their place is an elegant collection of buildings. A magnificent new concert hall seats 3000 people. The biggest dome ever built covers the Dome of Discovery. It is like a mushroom on thin legs. There is a crazy railway and a children's zoo. The tall thin needle is called the Skylon. It is lit up at night, and is a symbol of the future. The Festival Gardens and funfair are extremely popular. This is the first large leisure park in Britain.

The Festival of Britain site with the Skylon

BELGIANS WELCOME KING BAUDOUIN

July 16, Brussels King Leopold III of the Belgians has abdicated (resigned). The Belgians think he should not have surrendered to the Germans in 1940. There have been riots and strikes against him. His very popular first wife, Queen Astrid, died in a car crash in 1935. Her elder son will become King Baudouin I.

NORTH KOREANS PUSHED BACK

July 10, Korea Talks are going on to try to end the Korean war. All through the first months of this year battles raged in South Korea. By April the UN army had forced the North Koreans and Chinese back over the 38th parallel.

President Truman dismissed General MacArthur because he wanted to march his men into China. Such action might start a third world war. Casualties in Korea are heavy, and include hundreds of civilians.

SPANIARDS WANT THEIR ROCK BACK

Aug 5, Barcelona Today has been proclaimed Gibraltar Day. Gibraltar has been a British possession since the 17th century. This angers the Spanish, who say that it is part of Spain. They will mark this day every year until they get the Rock back.

CHURCHILL BACK IN PARLIAMENT

Oct 26, London   The British people have voted for a Conservative government. Mr. Winston Churchill is Prime Minister once more. Under the Labour government of 1945–51, many industries were nationalized. The Conservatives may return some of them to private companies.

Mrs. Churchill laughs as her husband Winston gives his famous victory salute.

PERÓN BACK IN POWER

Nov 11, Buenos Aires, Argentina   Colonel Juan Perón has been re-elected President of Argentina. He first came to power in 1945. Perón is very popular with working people. His wife Eva (Evita) has worked tirelessly among them. Her influence has won him many votes at election time. But the economy of the country is weak, and Perón has an added burden: his wife is very ill with cancer.

Juan and Eva Perón wave to the crowd at Buenos Aires.

NEWS IN BRIEF . . .

FAMILY LIFE TODAY

Sept 30, New York and London   Many towns are spreading outwards as houses are built in the suburbs. In America, new houses are being fitted with central heating for the first time. The heating is fuelled by oil or by gas. Suburban homes are bought by young couples with children. Usually the husband goes out to work while his wife looks after the children and does the housework. Many more people are marrying young these days.

GOOD FAMILY ENTERTAINMENT

Dec 15, New York   Singing cowboy Gene Autry has swept to fame with a song that is out just in time for Christmas. It is called 'Rudolf the Red-Nosed Reindeer'. Home entertainment is booming. The number of TV sets has increased. As a result 3000 cinemas have had to close. The movie industry has to produce better films to keep its audience. This year Marilyn Monroe has made *The Asphalt Jungle* and Bette Davis stars in *All About Eve*. In America you can visit a drive-in cinema. From your car, you can watch the movie on a huge screen.

On a night out at a drive-in movie

1952

MAU MAU IN KENYA
AFRICANS WANT MORE LAND

Jan 1, Nairobi At the beginning of this century, British settlers were given farms in Kenya. They enclosed their lands and would not allow strangers onto them. This is against African custom. Africans say that land belongs to everyone. Their population has increased, partly because of European medicine. Available land has become scarce.

A group of black nationalists has formed the Kenya African Union (KAU). They want the white government to give Africans more land. The nationalists sing a song which, translated, means: 'Mother, whether you cry or not, I will only come back when our lands are returned; when I obtain our lands and African freedom.'

OATH-TAKING IN KIKUYULAND

Aug 24, Nairobi A secret society called Mau Mau is recruiting Africans of the Kikuyu tribe. Recruits are forced to swear an oath that they will murder people if asked to. The Kikuyu believe that oaths are very powerful, and they will die if they break one. Most recruits are too frightened to protest. Oath-givers are touring the Kikuyu districts near Nairobi, recruiting for Mau Mau.

FUNERAL OF KIKUYU CHIEF

Oct 14, Nairobi Sir Evelyn Baring (the Governor of Kenya), Jomo Kenyatta (the President of the KAU), and members of the government were among the hundreds of mourners at the funeral of Kikuyu Chief Waruhiu. A week ago three gunmen shot him dead. Police believe the gunmen were Mau Mau, who have already murdered over 40 Kikuyu. A few days before his death Chief Waruhiu condemned Mau Mau violence.

Jomo Kenyatta (in light trousers) pictured at the funeral ceremony of Chief Waruhiu. Mr. Kenyatta is President of the KAU and is also suspected of being a Mau Mau leader.

STATE OF EMERGENCY IN KENYA

Oct 21, Nairobi Sir Evelyn Baring has declared a State of Emergency. British troops are coming to Kenya. They will search for the Mau Mau, who are living rough in the forests and hills. Others who have taken the oath stay in the towns. They supply the terrorists with food and information. Town-dwellers suspected of being Mau Mau have been rounded up.

Jomo Kenyatta has been arrested. The government thinks that the KAU is organizing Mau Mau.

British troops guard Kenyan villagers during a search for hidden Mau Mau weapons.

SAD NEWS REACHES KENYA

Feb 6, Nairobi Princess Elizabeth learnt tonight of the death of her father, King George VI. She has become Queen Elizabeth II of England. The Princess and Prince Philip arrived last night at the famous 'Treetops' lodge in Kenya. Armed game wardens protected the couple from a herd of elephants as they walked through the forest to the tree-house. During the night they saw in a floodlit clearing two waterbuck fighting each other to the death. Treetops' visitors book records that on this day a young woman climbed into the tree as a princess, and climbed down from the tree a queen.

PROMINENT WEST GERMAN ABDUCTED

July 8, West Berlin Berlin is surrounded by East Germany. The city is divided between the Russians, the Americans, the French and the British. Dr. Walter Linse, a lawyer living in Berlin, has told people about the cruelty taking place in East Germany. Today Dr. Linse was kidnapped in broad daylight. He was shot in the leg and bundled into a car. East German guards at the border closed the barrier after the kidnap car had passed.

The East Germans have put up double barbed wire fences along the frontier with West Germany.

Princess Elizabeth and the Duke of Edinburgh at the Sagana River in the Kenyan highlands

KING FAROUK TOLD TO LEAVE

July 23, Cairo   There has been a coup in Egypt. A group of young army officers has deposed King Farouk. Their leader is called Jamal Abd al-Nasser. King Farouk lived in luxury, and did not tackle his country's problems.

The rebels have set up a Revolutionary Council. General Neguib, head of the armed forces, will lead it. The Council will expel Europeans from top government jobs. They want the British army to leave the Suez Canal Zone. The British are alarmed at these decisions.

HEROES OF THE OLYMPICS

Aug 3, Helsinki   On July 19 a 55-year-old runner lit the Olympic torch to open the Olympic Games. The Finns gave him a great welcome. In 1920 and 1924 he was their Olympic hero. His name is Paavo Nurmi.

The Russians took part in the games for the first time since 1912. Two of their female competitors won gold medals. But this year's hero was Emil Zatopek of Czechoslovakia. He created Olympic records for the marathon, and the 10,000 and 5000 metre events. His wife Dana won the medal for women's javelin throwing.

A young woman dressed in white tried to take advantage of this meeting of East and West. At the opening ceremony she ran forward to plead for world peace. She was turned away from the microphone, her message unspoken.

SCHOOLBOY BECOMES KING

Aug 11, London   Crown Prince Hussein is 15 years old, and at school in England. Today he has become the King of Jordan. His grandfather, King Abdallah, was shot dead in Jerusalem a year ago. He created the state of Jordan from the old Transjordan and central Palestine. The new King wants to finish his education in Britain. Until he returns home, Jordan will be ruled by a council of three people.

NEW BOMB WILL BE DEADLY

Nov 30, Washington   United States scientists wore special dark glasses to watch tests on a new atomic bomb. The bomb is hundreds of times more powerful than those dropped on Japan in 1945. It is called an H-bomb (H is for hydrogen). Radioactive dust rose in a huge cloud 40 km (24 miles) high and 160 km (100 miles) wide. The tests were carried out on an uninhabited island in the Pacific. After the explosion, the island had completely disappeared. The Russians may also be working on an H-bomb. In the West, some people are building bomb shelters in their gardens.

The newly-crowned King on a visit to Rome

NEWS IN BRIEF . . .

OPERA GAINS A NEW WORK

Feb 28, London Benjamin Britten conducted his new opera, *Billy Budd*, this month at Covent Garden Opera House. The opera takes place on board an 18th-century naval ship. It tells the sad story of a sailor who accidentally kills an officer who is tormenting him. The tenor Peter Pears sings the leading role.

THE MOUSETRAP OPENS

Nov 25, London *The Mousetrap* opened last night in the West End. Agatha Christie, the author, has already written many detective novels. In this play, she keeps the audience guessing to the last. The detective, who works out which of many snow-bound characters had the motive, the means and the opportunity, is played by Richard Attenborough. Sheila Sim plays a leading role. If you want to know 'who-dunnit', you will have to go along to the Ambassador's Theatre and find out.

AMERICAN IS WORLD CHAMPION

Sept 24, Philadelphia Rocky Marciano is the new world heavy-weight boxing champion. Last night he knocked out 'Jersey' Joe Walcott after 13 rounds. In the first round Rocky was behind on points. But he recovered, and used his hard-hitting technique to batter the former champion. Rocky learnt to box in the army during the war. Before he took up boxing seriously, his first love was baseball.

3-D MOVIES HERE TO STAY?

Nov 26, Los Angeles Film-goers have to wear special glasses to see the latest movie, *B'wana Devil*. One lens is red, the other green. The glasses make the film seem to be three-dimensional. This could cause panic – in *B'wana Devil* lions appear to leap out of the screen! We shall see whether 3-D movies catch on, or if this is just a new gimmick.

LONDON'S AIR CAN KILL

Nov 31, London November is always a bad month for fog. But we now have 'smog'. The mixture of fog and smoke from factories and home coal fires is causing alarm. It is killing old people, young children, and those with asthma. The government is looking for ways of stopping this deadly form of air pollution.

UNUSUAL FISH IS RARE SURVIVAL FROM STONE AGE

Dec 29, Madagascar A fisherman has caught a very strange fish in the Indian Ocean. It is called a coelacanth. Fossil remains of the fish have been found in rocks. Scientists thought the fish became extinct about 50 million years ago!

1953

FIRST YEAR OF A NEW REIGN
PREPARATIONS FOR GREAT DAY

May 30, London Everyone is preparing for the Queen's coronation. The streets of London are decorated. Ten thousand servicemen have practised marching in procession. Two thousand bandsmen are perfecting their music, and 250 police horses are groomed daily. Overseas politicians and colonial rulers are arriving in London. Queen Elizabeth has asked for the route to be longer than usual so that more children can see the procession. Queen Elizabeth and Prince Philip have two children, Prince Charles and Princess Anne.

THE QUEEN IS CROWNED

June 2, London The New Elizabethan Age began today when Queen Elizabeth II was crowned in Westminster Abbey. Her golden coach was drawn by eight white horses. At the climax of the long ceremony, the Archbishop of Canterbury put the crown on her head. One royal visitor pleased the London crowd above all others. This was Queen Salote of Tonga, an island in the Pacific. Her warm personality and beaming smile drew cheers from the onlookers.

All over the country people are attending street parties and band concerts. In the evening most towns have dances and firework displays. It has been a cold rainy day, but this has not dampened the general excitement.

CLIMBERS ON ROOF OF THE WORLD

May 29, Nepal At 11.30 this morning two climbers made history. Edmund Hillary of New Zealand, and Tenzing Norgay of Nepal have reached the summit of Mount Everest. Sir John Hunt led the party of 10 British and 36 Nepalese climbers. Yesterday Hillary and Tenzing camped at a point nearly 9000 metres (27,900 ft) up the mountain. The temperature was −27°C, and the wind rose at times to gale force. At the top of Everest, Tenzing buried gifts of food to the god of the mountain, and Hillary buried a small crucifix.

Edmund Hillary (left) and Tenzing Norgay on Everest

ROYAL COUPLE TOUR COMMONWEALTH

Dec 25, Auckland, New Zealand The Queen broadcast her Christmas message to the Commonwealth today from New Zealand. She and Prince Philip have been away from England for over a month. They started their tour in the West Indies. On the Pacific island of Tonga they met Queen Salote again. The royal couple will visit Australia, Aden and Uganda. In May they will board *Britannia* in the Mediterranean for the journey home.

THE VIEW FROM EVEREST

'I was beginning to tire a little now. I had been cutting steps continuously for two hours and Tenzing, too, was moving very slowly . . . I wondered rather dully just how long we could keep it up. . . I then realized that the ridge ahead, instead of still monotonously rising, now dropped sharply away. . A few more whacks of the ice-axe in the firm snow and we stood on top.

My initial feelings were of relief – relief that there were no more steps to cut – no more ridges to traverse and no more humps to tantalize us with hopes of success. I looked at Tenzing and in spite of the balaclava, goggles and oxygen mask all encrusted with long icicles that concealed his face, there was no disguising his infectious grin of pure delight as he looked all around him. We shook hands and then Tenzing threw his arm around my shoulders and we thumped each other on the back until we were almost breathless. It was 11.30 a.m.'

(Edmund Hillary, from *The Ascent of Everest* by John Hunt, Hodder & Stoughton 1953)

The royal couple with Queen Salote of Tonga, an island in the Pacific Ocean

NEW PRESIDENT RESISTS SOVIETS

Jan 13, Belgrade, Yugoslavia Josip Tito has become President of Yugoslavia. He is the country's first Communist president. Stalin wanted Yugoslavia to be under Soviet control. Tito has resisted him. Yugoslavia will remain a neutral country – though its policies are like those of the USSR.

AFRICAN LEADER IS EXILED

Nov 30, Kampala, Uganda The Kabaka (King) of Buganda, Mutesa II, has been forced to leave Uganda by the British. Buganda is the country of the Ganda people. It forms a quarter of the British territory of Uganda. When self-government comes, the Ganda want Buganda to be a separate country. They are furious that their King has been exiled.

President Tito of Yugoslavia at his villa home

TANKS HALT EAST GERMAN REVOLT

June 21, Berlin The East Germans live under Soviet rule. They have gone on strike against longer hours of work, and the low standard of living. Thousands of German prisoners of war are still in Russia. The rioters demanded their return. They tore down Communist flags in the city.

It is the first time a country has revolted against Soviet occupation. Usually people are too frightened to do so. The Russians have sent tanks into the streets of East Germany to restore order.

SCIENTISTS FIND 'SECRET OF LIFE'

April 25, Cambridge We have known for some years that our height, looks, brain power, and everything about us depends on our genes. We inherit our genes from our parents. J.D. Watson and F.H.C. Crick of the University of Cambridge have discovered that genes are made of a chemical called DNA. DNA has a structure like a twisted ladder, which splits in half when a cell divides.

Demonstrators in East Berlin attack Soviet tanks.

VILLAGERS MASSACRED IN KENYA

Sept 15, Lari village, Kenya After a long trial, Jomo Kenyatta has been sentenced to seven years hard labour. He denied he was leading the Mau Mau, and his arrest has not stopped their attacks. They have destroyed 150 schools and killed 32 teachers. Last night they murdered nearly 100 men, women and children by setting fire to a whole village.

Many Kikuyu are against the Mau Mau. They have joined the Kikuyu Guard to protect their families. They show great bravery, because Guard posts are obvious targets for Mau Mau attacks.

USSR HAS NO FIRM LEADER

Dec 23, Moscow Stalin's death on March 5 was followed by a power struggle in the USSR. At that time Lavrenti Beria, the chief of the secret police, had immense power. But so had other leaders, including Molotov, Malenkov and Khrushchev. Beria is the first one to 'disappear'. Malenkov accused him of being a Western spy and trying to seize power. Today he was executed. The Russians hardly care who finally becomes sole leader. Forced labour, concentration camps and the dreaded secret police still dominate their lives.

NEWS IN BRIEF . . .

SEARCHING THE SEA BED

Jan 15, Switzerland A 70-year-old Swiss scientist, Auguste Piccard, has dived in a bathyscaphe of his own design to the bottom of the Mediterranean. He reached a depth of 3.5 km (2 miles). The fish down there live in darkness. Professor Piccard has explored not only the depths but also the heights: 22 years ago he reached the stratosphere in a balloon.

THE STANLEY MATTHEWS FINAL

May 29, London From high on Everest, Hillary and Tenzing today tuned their radio to the BBC. They heard tremendous excitement coming from Wembley Stadium. Two minutes before the end of the match, the score in the FA Cup Final stood at 3–2 to Bolton Wanderers. Then suddenly Blackpool's Stanley Matthews put on a terrific spurt. And in that last two minutes his footwork allowed Blackpool to score two goals and win the cup. The crowd cheered itself hoarse.

CRIPPLING DISEASE ATTACKED

March 26, New York The most feared disease today is poliomielitis (polio). Many victims die. Some have to use an 'iron lung', which helps their paralysed lungs to breathe. Others are crippled for life. Now at last a scientist, Dr. J. Salk, has vaccinated a group of children, to prevent them getting the disease.

TV NEWS IN BLACK AND WHITE

June 3, London About 25 million people watched the Coronation on TV; from their homes, their pubs and clubs, or their community halls. People who waited in the streets from dawn to see the Queen pass said that they preferred live action: TV shows things in black and white – they saw the procession in colour!

Stanley Matthews after his team's victory in the FA Cup Final

1954

VIETNAM AND THE FRENCH

FRENCH HOLDING VIETNAM

Jan 1, Dien Bien Phu, Vietnam   Since 1945 the French have occupied a part of north Vietnam. Vietnamese Communists, the Viet Minh, want the French to leave. Their forces are led by General Giap. The country around Dien Bien Phu is mountainous, and thickly forested.

Last November the French dropped paratroops in the north-west of Vietnam, and captured Dien Bien Phu. They thought that guerrillas would come down in small groups from the mountains, and be easy targets to attack. But General Giap was cleverer than that. He has led a huge army to the outskirts of Dien Bien Phu. His soldiers even dragged field guns over the mountains. And 20,000 men with equipment on bicycles followed through the narrow jungle paths. It is clear that General Giap means to oust the French garrison from their stronghold position.

VIET MINH ENTER TOWN

May 8, Dien Bien Phu   After a siege lasting 55 days, the French have finally been defeated by the Viet Minh. The French garrison of about 19,000 men was completely surrounded. The French did not hold any of the territory round Dien Bien Phu, so there was nowhere for them to go. Those who survived the siege surrendered to General Giap's North Vietnamese troops. It seems that after this heavy defeat, France has no future in Indo-China.

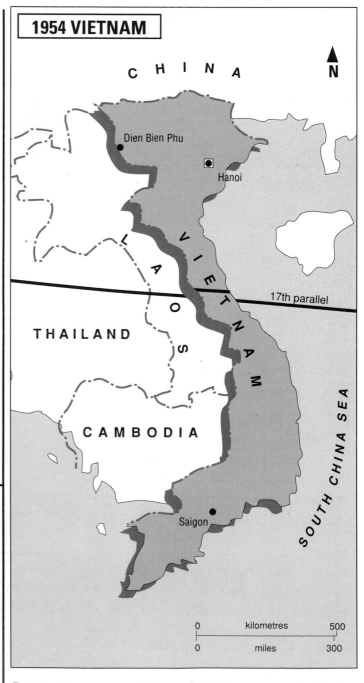

1954 VIETNAM

During the course of this year, Vietnam was divided into two countries.

VIETNAM TO BE DIVIDED

July 21, Geneva   The United Nations has ruled that Vietnam should be divided into two countries. The northern part, where all the fighting has taken place, is to be called North Vietnam. Its capital will be Hanoi. Ho Chi Minh, the Communist leader of the Viet Minh, will be its President. His rule will end at latitude 17°, the '17th parallel'. South of this is South Vietnam. It will be ruled by Emperor Bao Dai. The French will support his government.

Ho Chi Minh, leader of the Viet Minh

FAMILIES MOVE TO THE SOUTH

Oct 8, Vietnam   Thousands of refugees are leaving North Vietnam and going to the South. President Eisenhower of the United States has sent American ships to transport them by sea. He says that Communist gains in south-east Asia have 'a domino effect': when one country falls, the second, third and fourth need less and less pressure to fall too. He does not like to see a Communist government in North Vietnam.

THE WITCH-HUNT IS OVER

Dec 2, Washington   Mr. McCarthy's fellow Senators have finally turned against him. He has called too many innocent people Communist, or un-American. In the past four years he has charged two presidents with treason, threatened the army chiefs, and recruited hundreds of anti-Communist spies. Because of him 600 college professors have been dismissed.

SEATO AIDS PEACEFUL DEVELOPMENT

Sept 8, Manila, Philippines   Eight countries have agreed to join together to keep the peace in south-east Asia. They will also send south-east Asian countries money for their development. The members of SEATO (South-East Asia Treaty Organization) are the United States, Britain, France, Pakistan, Australia, New Zealand, Thailand and the Philippines. They will meet next year.

TROOPS TO LEAVE SUEZ

July 27, Cairo   The British have agreed that troops will leave the Suez Canal Zone over the next two years. They will only return if a Middle Eastern country tries to invade Egypt. The agreement was signed with Colonel Nasser, who has taken over from General Neguib. Last May he declared the country a republic. His policy to end imperialism is known to all Egyptians; his new radio station broadcasts his socialist and anti-Western views.

British troops beside the Suez Canal

MAU MAU REVENGE ATTACK

May 26, Nairobi, Kenya 'Treetops', which the Queen visited last year, has been burnt to the ground. One of Treetops' lorry-drivers was a member of Mau Mau. For several months he drove food and other supplies into the forest. Armed Africans were waiting. They took the supplies to the Mau Mau in the mountains. When the British discovered this, they tried to ambush the armed men. The ambush failed. The Mau Mau took their revenge by burning the tourist lodge. Royal Air Force planes are trying to bomb the Mau Mau out of the Aberdares mountain range.

THE POWER OF A NUCLEAR BLAST

June 29, Washington Last month the United States exploded another H-bomb. The test took place on the island of Bikini. The bomb's power was so great that fishermen in a boat 112 km (68 miles) away were badly affected by radiation sickness.

People all over the world are extremely frightened in case war breaks out between two countries with H-bombs. The leading American scientist, Dr. Robert Oppenheimer, would like to ban them. He helped to develop nuclear bombs. Now he is no longer allowed to work on atomic projects because of his views.

NEWS IN BRIEF . . .

ATHLETE IN FOUR-MINUTE MILE

May 6, Oxford For years runners have been trying to run a mile in less than four minutes. Today 25-year-old Roger Bannister has set a new record of 3 minutes 59.4 seconds. He is very interested in the whole subject of running – how to get the best out of yourself. He trains carefully.

The record-breaking moment as Roger Bannister crosses the winning line.

RABBITS MUST GO, SAY FARMERS

June 30, Britain Farmers hate rabbits. They damage young trees, and nibble grass down to ground level. When this happens, moss takes over, and sheep won't eat moss.

But now the rabbits have a deadly enemy. It is a virus called myxomatosis. It is killing thousands of rabbits. Although they have to be controlled, it is distressing to see them suffering from this disease.

YOU CAN BUY FOOD FREELY NOW

July 3, London Food rationing has finally ended. You may burn your ration books! Shops are now more plentifully stocked, and luxury items are returning to the shelves. We seem to be eating less red meat and more chicken. We eat less sugar than before the war – even though sweets have not been rationed for a year. There are some new imported fruits in the shops, and more people are drinking coffee.

WHERE WINE FLOWS LIKE WATER

Oct 15, France The grape harvest is attracting a lot of casual labour. The grapes are made into wine, which is one of France's most famous exports. It is also a Frenchman's daily drink. Doctors say a man should drink no more than one litre of red wine a day. Many drink a lot more than that, especially in rural areas. The government is starting a campaign to warn people of the danger of heavy drinking.

1955

CIVIL WAR IN CYPRUS
ISLANDERS WANT UNION WITH GREECE

Jan 1, Nicosia, Cyprus   The island of Cyprus is ruled by the British. Although it lies just south of Turkey, more Greeks live here than Turks. Cypriot Greeks want Cyprus to be part of Greece. They call this union *enosis*. Five years ago they gained a powerful leader. He is Archbishop Makarios, head of the Greek Church in Cyprus. Athens radio encourages Cypriot Greeks to fight for *enosis*.

FIGHTING BREAKS OUT IN CYPRUS

June 30, Nicosia   A Greek army officer, Colonel George Grivas, has recruited hundreds of young Greeks into a guerrilla army. They are called EOKA, which in Greek stands for National Organization of Cypriot Struggle. They are burning buildings in Nicosia, the capital of the country, and in the eastern town of Famagusta. A large number of Turkish civilians have been murdered, and their homes and farms destroyed.

BRITISH IN CONFLICT WITH EOKA

Nov 28, Nicosia   The British government has declared a state of emergency in Cyprus. This means that the Governor may deport or arrest anyone who disturbs the peace. Only the British may be armed. This comes after months of heavy fighting. British commando troops were flown in. They have been searching for guerrillas in the mountains. Hundreds have already been arrested. If they are convicted of planting bombs or of murder they are executed.

There is still intense fighting in the streets of Famagusta. The troops are calling this the 'Murder mile'. The British blame Archbishop Makarios for supporting Colonel Grivas and the EOKA. This is one more British territory that is causing trouble. But if the British leave, the Greeks and Turks will still be at loggerheads. The British government hopes to solve the crisis before withdrawing.

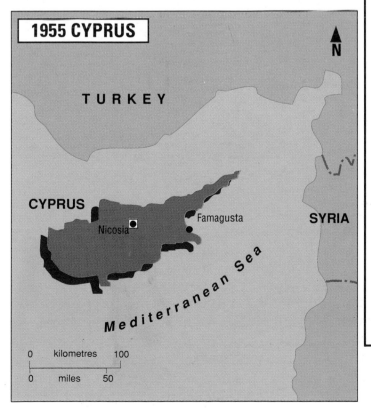

1955 CYPRUS

N

TURKEY

CYPRUS

Nicosia   Famagusta   SYRIA

Mediterranean Sea

0   kilometres   100
0   miles   50

Although close to Turkey, Cyprus is a largely Greek island, under British rule.

THE WARSAW PACT SIGNED

May 14, Warsaw   The Soviet Union and seven other Eastern European countries have made a pact to help one another. If one country is attacked, the rest will go to its defence. But they are agreed that disarmament is necessary for world peace. The Russians organized the Pact as an association similar to NATO, the alliance to which Western countries belong. The headquarters of the Warsaw Pact is in Moscow.

The Warsaw Pact committee with Soviet ministers Marshall Zhukov, Mr. Molotov and Marshall Konyev of the joint armed forces

BLACK AMERICANS BOYCOTT BUSES

Dec 5, Montgomery, Alabama   Black Americans have sworn to walk or cycle to work instead of going by bus. Last Thursday a young black dressmaker got on a bus after doing her Christmas shopping. The back of the bus, where blacks are supposed to sit, was full. She sat in a 'whites' only' seat. As the bus filled, the driver called "Niggers move back". The young lady stayed where she was. She was arrested and fined.

Over the weekend a young black clergyman, Dr. Martin Luther King, organized a bus boycott. Nobody knows much about him, but his message is love and understanding: "Don't ever let anyone pull you so low as to make you hate them," he says. The boycott is attracting attention all over the United States, as a form of peaceful protest.

PRINCESS MARGARET NOT TO MARRY

Oct 31, London   Princess Margaret's romance with Group Captain Peter Townsend is over. She has decided not the marry the former airforce officer. Members of the royal family do not usually marry without the Queen's consent. Peter Townsend is divorced, and this would make it difficult for the Queen to give her consent. She is Head of the Anglican Church, whose marriage service contains the words 'till death us do part'. If Princess Margaret had married Townsend she would have given up her place as third in line to the throne.

Princess Margaret with Group Captain Townsend in South Africa

SOUTH VIETNAM IS A REPUBLIC

Oct 26, Saigon   The Emperor of South Vietnam, Bao Dai, lives in the south of France. He left the government of the country to his ministers. In April rebels started a civil war in Saigon, the capital. They defeated the government, and today they declared South Vietnam a republic. Its first president is Ngo Dinh Diem.

BURGESS AND MACLEAN NEWS

Sept 18, London A Russian has published an article in a British newspaper. It is about the missing Foreign Office men, Guy Burgess and Donald Maclean. They are in the Soviet Union. The article claims they were recruited as Russian spies while they were at Cambridge University in the 1930s. Nobody has discovered yet who is the 'third man' who warned them to leave England.

Guy Burgess

Donald Maclean

NEWS IN BRIEF . . .

LITTLE MO IS TO RETIRE

Feb 22, New York Maureen Connolly is going to retire from tennis championships. She was only 16 when in 1951 she won the US women's tennis tournament. Little Mo, as she was called, also drew crowds to Wimbledon's centre court. She won the women's singles three years in succession. During those years she also won three US championships. Little Mo is a great horse rider. But last year she had a fall and injured her leg. She has not played in tennis tournaments since then. Now she plans to coach other players.

ACTOR KILLED IN ROAD ACCIDENT

Sept 30, Los Angeles James Dean was the hero of countless teenage movie fans. He has died today in a car crash at the age of 24. His latest film has not yet been released. Called *Rebel Without a Cause*, it is about a rich young man who is angry and frustrated with life. James Dean's death brings to an end a promising career, which began with a part in the film *East of Eden*.

THIS YEAR'S FASHION TIP

July 31, London Young men are rebelling against traditional gear. They choose clothes that copy those of King Edward VII's day – which is why they are called 'Teddy boys'. There is a brisk trade in long jackets with velvet collars, brocade waistcoats, bootlace ties, narrow trousers and 'winkle-picker' shoes. 'Teds' let their hair grow long and leave their sideburns intact.

Mary Quant's new shop called Bazaar in Chelsea sells straight shifts in synthetic materials for the girls. They wear them with plastic costume jewellery. And a new fashion has arrived from America – skin-tight jeans. Jeans were first worn by miners in the United States, but here it is the girls who are buying and wearing them.

Teddy boys in London

IT PAYS TO ADVERTISE

Sept 22, London At 8.15 p.m. you will be able to see the first ever advertisement to appear on British television. It encourages you to buy Gibbs SR toothpaste, and shows a toothbrush and toothpaste tube in a block of ice. Viewers are looking forward to watching the new independent channel (ITV).

CROCKETT BOOM ENDS

Dec 15, London The craze for Davy Crockett hats is over. Christmas shoppers are looking for other attractions. The trade in coon-skins boomed for six months as children dressed like their hero. The real Davy Crockett was an American hunter who died in 1836. His picture shows him dressed in a fur hat with a tail. Now the King of the Wild Frontier is becoming just a legend once more.

1956

July 26   Nasser nationalizes Suez Canal
Oct 17   Britain's first nuclear power plant opens
Oct 30   Israelis march on Egypt
Oct 31   Hungarians fight for freedom
Nov 5   Soviet tanks crush Hungary
Nov 21   UN troops arrive at Suez

THE SUEZ CRISIS

NASSER TAKES OVER CANAL

July 26, Suez, Egypt Colonel Nasser has nationalized the Suez Canal. He announced this after Britain and America decided not to pay for Egypt's new Aswan Dam. With the money the canal earns, the Egyptians will be able to pay for the dam themselves. The British and French say that Nasser's action is unlawful.

PILOTS WALK OUT

Sept 14, Suez Today British and French pilots walked out of their jobs on the Suez Canal. The Egyptians have only a few trained pilots of their own. It is a highly specialized job. The Egyptian pilots say that they will work long hours without extra pay. They will train new recruits. Colonel Nasser says he will never use foreign pilots again.

ISRAELIS THREATEN EGYPT

Oct 30, Suez Yesterday Israeli troops marched towards the canal from the east. They said they were trying to stop the Egyptians raiding Israeli territory. The British and French demanded that both Israelis and Egyptians withdraw, leaving a no-man's-land of 16 km (10 miles) on each side of the canal. The Israelis have agreed, but the Egyptians have not. Some people think the British government encouraged the Israelis to invade.

EGYPTIANS BLOCK THE CANAL

Nov 6, Suez The Egyptians have sunk several ships in the canal, and completely blocked it. All ships will now have to travel right round Africa. This adds 10,000 km (6000 miles) to their journey.

British aircraft have bombed military targets in Egypt. The British and French dropped paratroops in the area. The Israelis are again advancing towards the canal. The United Nations has asked all foreign troops to leave Egypt at once.

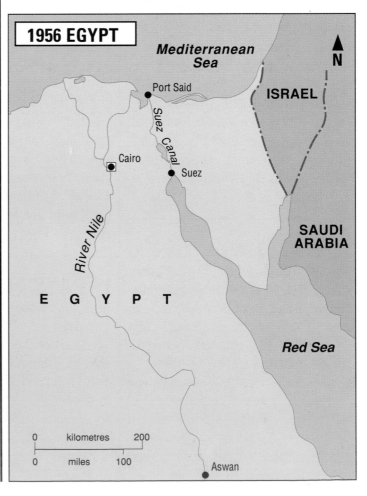

1956 EGYPT

28

HUNGARY FIGHTS FOR FREEDOM

Oct 31, Budapest, Hungary Last week a huge crowd of people gathered in Budapest's main square. They demanded that Russian troops leave Hungary. Since the war Russian secret police have been spying on Hungarians. Nobody had any freedom of speech or action. Now people have brought out national flags that have been hidden for years. They have destroyed a huge bronze statue of Stalin in the city centre.

Rioters entered the prison and freed Cardinal Mindszenty, the head of the Roman Catholic Church in Hungary. He was sentenced by the Russians to life imprisonment in 1949.

Demonstrators in Hungary pulled down a huge statue of Stalin.

RUSSIANS RETURN IN FORCE

Nov 5, Budapest After just five days of freedom, Hungary is once again under the Russian heel. Yesterday Soviet planes bombed the centre of Budapest. A thousand tanks flattened houses and fired on civilians. Mr. Khrushchev says that the troops were invited back by loyal Hungarian Communists.

The Hungarians fought bitterly and bravely, but they did not have the power to resist. Cardinal Mindszenty is safe in the American Embassy. Professional guides are charging high prices to lead over 200,000 refugees across the border into Yugoslavia and Austria. The route to freedom is dangerous because it is heavily mined.

UN FORCES ARRIVE AT SUEZ

Nov 21, Suez A United Nations peace-keeping force has arrived at Suez to take over control of the region. It will take several months before the canal can be used again. The Americans blame the British for handling the affair badly.

The first UN troops arrive in Port Said, Egypt.

EX-CHIEF RETURNS TO AFRICA

April 8, Gaberones, Bechuanaland Seretse Khama has returned to the country of his birth, Bechuanaland [Botswana]. In 1948 he married an English girl, Ruth Williams. The marriage dismayed his people, the Bamangwato. Seretse Khama was going to be their chief. How could his son, who would be half English, succeed him? To avoid trouble, the British rulers exiled Seretse Khama from Bechuanaland. He now says he will give up the Chieftainship. Ruth Khama is very happy to be returning to her adopted country.

CYPRUS LOSES ARCHBISHOP MAKARIOS

May 25, Nicosia In March the British government deported Archbishop Makarios to the Seychelles, in the Indian Ocean. The British would like to give Cyprus self-government – but there must first be peace between Cypriot Greeks and Turks. Greece supports EOKA, the Greek nationalists' army; Turkey supports the Cypriot Turks. Greece and Turkey could go to war over who owns the island.

POWER FOR THE FUTURE

Oct 17, Cumbria Britain's first nuclear power station was opened today by Her Majesty the Queen. It is at Calder Hall in Cumbria. It will provide electricity. Our usual sources of energy, coal and gas, may be finished within 200 years. It is therefore important to begin using other sources now.

Calder Hall nuclear power station in Cumbria

STUDENTS STAGE FREEDOM MARCH

Nov 29, Barcelona, Spain There have been student demonstrations in Spain. The students carried placards saying WE ARE AGAINST DICTATORSHIP – and below – FOR HUNGARY. They are really against General Franco's dictatorship in their own country. Everybody is under state control. Spaniards have to work harder than other Europeans for less pay. They cannot afford much to eat. They take great risks when they demonstrate against the state. Thousands of Spaniards have been imprisoned without trial.

COUNTRIES BOYCOTT OLYMPICS

Dec 8, Melbourne, Australia The Duke of Edinburgh opened the 16th Olympic Games – and the first to be held 'down under'. Several countries decided not to join in this year. They are protesting against Russia's invasion of Hungary, and Britain's and France's treatment of Egypt. But three African countries were represented for the first time: they are Kenya, Malawi and Ethiopia. Australian women performed well, though Britain's Judy Grinham won the 100m backstroke.

Chris Brasher of Britain wins the 3000m Steeplechase.

COLD WAR THAWS A LITTLE

April 26, London Mr. Khrushchev has been visiting Britain for talks with the Prime Minister, Sir Anthony Eden. Though the East and the West cannot agree, Mr. Khrushchev said, they could respect each other's point of view. There could be 'peaceful co-existence' between the two. This is seen as a softening of the Soviet hard-line policy toward the West. But in America, the Secretary of State said the United States must be prepared to go to the brink of war.

In February Mr. Khrushchev denounced Stalin. He said he was a brutal murderer. Perhaps people will be able to live happier lives now the truth is out. Some political prisoners have been freed.

Sir Anthony Eden (left) and Mr. Khrushchev shake hands at No. 10 Downing Street.

NEWS IN BRIEF . . .

ACTRESSES MARRY

June 29, Hollywood Today glamorous film star Marilyn Monroe married playwright Arthur Miller. His latest play, *The Crucible*, is about a witch-hunt in 17th-century America. It was first staged while Senator McCarthy was engaged on his modern witch-hunt of Communists. Marilyn will soon be off to London to film *The Prince and the Showgirl* with British actor Sir Lawrence Olivier.

In April, the beautiful American actress Grace Kelly married her Prince Charming. He is Prince Rainier of Monaco, a tiny country on the Mediterranean, between France and Italy. Grace's last film, *To Catch a Thief*, may have shown her a taste of the future. Its setting is the luxury French Riviera.

Wedding belles: Marilyn Monroe and husband Arthur Miller, above, and below, Grace Kelly, who is now Princess of Monaco.

NEW PLAY AT EDINBURGH FESTIVAL

Sept, Edinburgh One of Dylan Thomas's last works was a radio play called *Under Milk Wood*. It has now been made into a stage play. The play tells of a day in the life of a Welsh seaside village called Llaregub. It is full of comic, tender and sad characters and situations. It was first heard on the radio in 1954, narrated by Richard Burton. Just three months before, Dylan Thomas had died in New York.

FIGHT FOR FRENCH WOMEN'S RIGHTS

Oct 31, Grenoble, France A law passed 36 years ago makes family planning illegal in France. An enterprising woman is fighting the law. She has opened a birth-control clinic in Grenoble. Women have fewer rights in France than in England or America. A married woman even has to have her husband's permission to open a bank account.

1957

MIXED-RACE SCHOOLING RIOTS

SCHOOL ACCEPTS BLACK PUPILS

Sept 1, Little Rock, Arkansas   In the Southern states of America, blacks and whites have in the past attended different schools. This is changing in most states. But in Arkansas black and white children are not allowed to play games together – not even dominoes! Some teachers are speaking out against this law. In Little Rock, the school board has accepted nine black pupils for next term, three boys and six girls.

GOVERNOR SENDS IN THE GUARDS

Sept 2, Little Rock   The Governor of Arkansas surrounded Little Rock Central School with 270 National Guards today. Term begins tomorrow. The Governor says he wants to avoid trouble. But his action seems to invite a fight.

GUARDS REFUSE CHILDREN ENTRY

Sept 4, Little Rock   Two black and two white church leaders walked with the nine black pupils to school. The National Guard turned them away. So they walked back calmly and bravely through a huge mob of jeering whites. Americans in more liberal states are ashamed of the whites' behaviour.

National Guardsmen are posted outside this school at Little Rock on the Governor's orders.

PRESIDENT SENDS IN TROOPS

Sept 24, Little Rock   Yesterday the black students succeeded in entering Little Rock school. President Eisenhower has denounced the Governor of Arkansas. He has sent 1100 army paratroopers to Little Rock. He has also made the National Guard into a state police force. This means the Governor cannot give the Guard orders.

VICTORY HARD FOR BLACKS

Sept 30, Little Rock   The nine pupils are showing great courage. They are escorted to and from school by soldiers. Many of their schoolmates are unkind and insulting. But they are determined to stay. The Governor is furious, and many of his white voters are on his side. The fight for black rights in the south is not yet won.

CONSERVATIVES LED BY MACMILLAN

Jan 10, London   Sir Anthony Eden retired after the Suez crisis. Britain's new prime minister is Mr. Harold Macmillan. He backed Eden's policy in Suez. Now he will have to win the Americans round.

Conservative Prime Minister Mr. Harold Macmillan

SIX COUNTRIES IN ECONOMIC UNION

March 25, Rome   Six Western nations today joined together to form a Common Market. The nations are France, West Germany, Italy, Belgium, Holland and Luxemburg. After the events in Hungary, they wish for a stronger central Europe. The six nations will allow their people to move freely between member countries. They will not tax each others' exports. Britain is not a member, though the six nations urged her to join them.

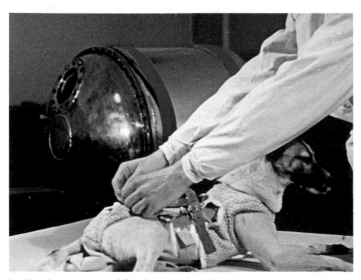

Laika is prepared for her space journey.

GOLD COAST BECOMES GHANA

March 7, Accra   There were joyful celebrations in Accra tonight. The Gold Coast is the first British colony to become an independent member of the British Commonwealth. The new President, Dr. Kwame Nkrumah, renamed the country 'Ghana'. (A previous Ghana in West Africa was a wealthy trading nation in the 11th century.) As the British flag came down, the new Ghanaians hoisted their own flag of red, yellow and green.

Dr. Nkrumah in the Ghanaian Legislative Assembly

RUSSIAN SPACE SUCCESS

Nov 2, Moscow   The Russians have launched the world's first artificial satellite. On October 4 an enormous rocket hurtled into space, carrying a sphere which is now circling the earth. It is called *Sputnik I*, and it weighs 83 kg (182 lb).

Now the Russians have put a much larger satellite, *Sputnik II*, into orbit. It is circling the earth at about 28,800 km an hour – with a dog called Laika on board. Laika is in a sealed container. She receives food at regular intervals. Machines record the effects of space travel on a living animal. Other instruments are measuring the sun's radiation, and sending signals back to earth. These signals have been picked up in many parts of the world.

Western scientists are amazed that such a large satellite could be sent into orbit. It weighs over 500 kg (half a ton).

NEWS IN BRIEF . . .

AMERICAN GIRL MAKES HISTORY

July 6, Wimbledon Althea Gibson's life has been made up of tennis 'firsts'. She was born 30 years ago in Harlem, New York. In 1950 she was the first black competitor in a tennis tournament at Forest Hills, in the United States. She was the first black lady to win Wimbledon doubles, the French singles and doubles, and the Italian singles. And she has crowned her career this week by winning both the singles and doubles championships at Wimbledon.

Miss Gibson, the number one seed at Wimbledon

THE BEAT GENERATION

June 2, San Francisco 'Beatniks' in khaki trousers, sandals and sweaters are the in-crowd in America. The men wear beards and the girls use heavy eyeshadow. Sometimes they smoke 'pot', but they don't go in for hard drugs. They see their way of life as a new religion. They say they love everybody and everything. Their talk is full of slang: 'chicks', 'dig', 'bread'. The word 'like' occurs in almost every sentence: 'Like it means nothing'; 'It's like cool'.

THE CONSUMER SOCIETY IS HERE

July 20, Britain "Most of our people have never had it so good", Mr. Harold Macmillan has said. Our parents and grandparents would be astonished to see our houses today. Washing machines, telephones, radios and refrigerators were real luxuries in the 1930s. The state looks after us better. We have sickness benefits, family allowances, and pensions.

RACING DRIVER BEATS OWN RECORD

August 4, Germany Juan Fangio has become the world car-racing champion by winning the German Grand Prix which is the toughest circuit in Europe. On the bumpy track tyres burst, mirrors fall off, and shock-absorbers become red hot. Last year Fangio drove a record lap in 9 minutes 41.6 seconds in a Lancia Ferrari. In this year's race, in a Maserati, his fastest lap was 9 minutes 17.4 seconds. Afterwards Fangio said, "I took myself and my car to the limit, and perhaps a little bit more."

SPACE EXPLORATION AND ENTERTAINMENT

Sept 26, London and New York Are we all space mad? Film-makers seem to think so. We have an endless diet of science fiction, evil aliens, mad scientists, shock and horror. The latest is *The Incredible Shrinking Man*. It follows *Invaders from Mars* and *Invasion of the Body Snatchers*.

West Side Story, a musical now showing in New York, brings us back to earth, and to the present. This is the story of a modern Romeo and Juliet. Leonard Bernstein's marvellous music accompanies teenage gang warfare and a haunting love story.

A scene from *West Side Story*

BRITONS DISCOVER COSTA DEL SOL

July 15, Madrid, Spain Tourism is a new industry in Spain. The Spaniards did not like it at first. Many of them are poor, and resent serving well-off holiday-makers. But tourists bring money to the country. Plots of land on the unspoiled Costa Brava are selling well. The rate of exchange is very much in the tourists' favour, making food and drink there very cheap.

1958

CIVIL WAR IN ALGERIA

ALGERIANS WANT SELF-GOVERNMENT

Jan 1, Algiers   Algeria has been a French colony for a hundred years. It has a million French settlers. Most native Algerians are Muslims. Many have to migrate to France to find work. There is none for them in Algeria.

Members of a political party, the National Liberation Front (FLN), want to get rid of the French settlers. They want self-government. For four years they have been fighting the French army and the settlers.

ALGERIA TO STAY FRENCH

Feb 5, Paris   The French parliament has voted for Algeria to remain a part of the French republic. They say that both Frenchmen and Algerian Muslims should take part in the Algerian government. The FLN are totally against this. They continue to fight for independence.

ATROCITIES IN NORTH AFRICA

Feb 12, Algiers   The Prime Minister of neighbouring Tunisia has asked French troops to leave Algeria. The French have bombed a Tunisian village just over the border. They thought FLN fighters were hiding there. The bombs killed and wounded 75 Tunisians, many of them children.

FRENCH SETTLERS SHOW STRENGTH

May 13, Algiers   There are now 500,000 French soldiers in Algeria. In the guerrilla fighting, casualties on both sides have been heavy. The army and the settlers are afraid that the French government will give in to the FLN. So today they seized government buildings, and business has come to a standstill. In Paris, people have been rioting in support of the settlers.

The French government is weak, and the war in Algeria is costing France more than it can afford. The settlers want General de Gaulle to take over. They are sure he would support them.

French troops near Algiers display the stock of arms seized in a recent battle with FLN fighters, 44 of whom were killed.

DE GAULLE SPEAKS TO ALGERIA

Oct 23, Paris   General de Gaulle became Premier of France in June. He has dashed the settlers' hopes of a French Algeria. He wants the country to be self-supporting, but with strong ties to France. He will see that 400,000 jobs are created for Algerians.

MANCHESTER LOSES HALF ITS TEAM

Feb 6, Munich, Germany   A horrific aircrash here today has killed seven members of Manchester United football team. They were on their way home from a match in Belgrade. The plane hit a fence and crashed into an airport building. Several journalists were also killed, and the team manager is badly hurt. The news has shocked the people of Manchester. The team would have played in the Cup Final in May.

The crashed Elizabethan aircraft at Munich airport, with snow still falling

NOBEL WINNER DENIED PRIZE

Dec 10, Stockholm, Sweden   Boris Pasternak has been awarded the Nobel Prize for Literature. His most recent book is *Dr Zhivago*. He could only publish it abroad, because of Russian censorship. The government of the USSR has banned his work and will not allow him to accept the prize.

MARCH AGAINST NUCLEAR WEAPONS

April 7, Aldermaston   The new Campaign for Nuclear Disarmament (CND) received publicity today when a crowd of 3000 arrived here from London. Many had walked all the way. Scientists at Aldermaston are developing new types of nuclear weapons. CND believes that the arms race is no way to ensure peace. The president of CND is the famous philosopher and writer, Bertrand Russell.

Demonstrators against the H-bomb march on Whitehall.

NEW SPACE AGENCY OPENED

July 29, Washington   The Americans want to catch up with the Russians in space exploration. The National Aeronautics and Space Agency (NASA) has been opened. It will carry out research on rockets and space craft. The US has two satellites in a higher orbit than that of the Russian Sputniks. One of them is making its own electricity from sunlight. They are small satellites, and their purpose is to record data about the earth and space.

MIDDLE EASTERN CRISIS ALARMS WEST

July 14, Baghdad, Iraq   Earlier this year Egypt and Syria became the United Arab Republic (UAR). Iraq and Jordan also united their two kingdoms. Now there has been a coup in Iraq. The 23-year-old King Feisal, his uncle, and his Prime Minister have all been murdered. Colonel Nasser of Egypt has backed the coup. King Hussein of Jordan is now afraid that the UAR, led by Nasser, may attack Jordan. The British and Americans are landing troops in Jordan. The Russians back the UAR. The two superpowers, America and the Soviet Union, are on opposite sides of a dangerous international conflict once again.

POPE WINS PRISONERS' FREEDOM

Nov 7, Barcelona   Three days ago the new pope, John XXIII, was crowned in Rome. Spain's General Franco announced that in honour of the occasion political prisoners would be released. Today over 16,000 men and women were set free and have joined their families. Many were imprisoned without trial, and on minor charges. There is no sign that General Franco's government will change its policy.

His Holiness Pope John XXIII

KHRUSHCHEV WANTS BERLIN FREE

Nov 30, Moscow   Mr. Khrushchev has got rid of all his rivals in the Kremlin. He is now looking towards East Germany. He says Berlin should be a 'free city'. West Berliners dread this possibility. The city, they say, would not be free for very long. The French, British and Americans are refusing to leave their zones of Berlin. Berlin is still an escape route for East Germans. Nearly a million have left the Communist East since 1952.

ELVIS HAS HIS MARCHING ORDERS

Mar 24, New York   Elvis Presley has been called up for his compulsory military service. The king of rock and roll has had his hair cut short. He can no longer wear the pink jackets and eye make-up that drive the girls wild. Friends say Elvis is just a quiet and polite country lad. He is also big business: his fans buy his records in millions.

Elvis Presley, the rock 'n roll star

NEWS IN BRIEF . . .

JET PLANES CARRY PASSENGERS

Oct 4, London Today the first passengers flew from London to New York in a jet plane, BOAC's Comet. Pan American plans to start a jet service with Boeing 707s before the end of the month. Up to now, most travellers between the two countries have sailed on luxury ocean-going liners. These famous ships may go out of business as air travel becomes faster.

Passengers enjoy luxury aboard the tourist cabin of a Comet.

CIRCLING IS GOOD FOR THE HIPS

Sept 30, London The latest craze to reach Europe from the United States is the hula-hoop. Spinning for health, for pleasure, to music, for the *Guinness Book of Records* – whatever people twirl the hoop for it is selling millions of these plastic rings.

In Paris's Champs-Elysées traffic came to a standstill when girls demonstrated the hula-hoop. They were dressed in bathing suits and accompanied by a Country and Western band!

THE LAST CURTSEYS

March 18, London Today the last débutantes were presented to the Queen. Every year 'debs' have made their curtseys at Court at the start of the social season in London, where these young ladies 'come out'. Nowadays this practice seems old-fashioned, and this year's crop of débutantes will be the last.

The tradition was also seen as taking up too much of Her Majesty's valuable time.

BEEHIVE HAIRSTYLES STAY PUT

Nov 30, London Girls are back-combing their hair and holding it high off the forehead with plenty of hairspray. The 'beehive' hairdo stays put! This style goes with pretty print dresses and high-heeled shoes.

HOW LONG DO WE LIVE?

Dec 31, London People can expect to live longer now than they did 18 years ago. In 1938 a man lived on average 58½ years, and a woman 63 years. Today the averages are 67½ years for a man, and 74 years for a woman.

1959

HEADING FOR SPACE
LUNA II SPEEDS TO THE SUN

Jan 12, Moscow The Russians have launched a rocket called *Luna II* towards the sun. It is the first rocket to escape earth's gravity. It will not return to the earth, but for some time it will send signals and information back.

NASA IS TRAINING ASTRONAUTS

May 28, Washington NASA is training seven men for the exciting but frightening task of being sent into space. The men will be called 'astronauts'. In specially designed chambers they are finding out what it is like to be weightless. They will not be sent into space until more tests are made with animal passengers. Today two monkeys returned safely after a 480-km (300-mile) journey into space.

ANOTHER 'FIRST' FOR USSR

Oct 27, Moscow This evening viewers of Moscow television saw the first extraordinary pictures of the other side of the moon – the side we never see. A Russian satellite, *Luna III*, was launched on October 4. Two days later it began to orbit the moon. A camera on the satellite took pictures for 40 minutes, and transmitted them to earth. Many of these pictures have been printed in the world's newspapers today. Russian scientists have already named eight features on the moon's far side.

DALAI LAMA SAFE IN INDIA

April 19, Lhasa, Tibet The Buddhist ruler of Tibet, the Dalai Lama, has been forced to leave his capital city, Lhasa, in disguise. When the Chinese marched into Tibet they promised to modernize the country, then leave. That was nine years ago, and they are still here. They have ruled the Tibetans harshly. Tibetan guerrillas are fighting the Chinese in the east. They have blown up bridges and mined roads. Chinese soldiers were told to capture the Dalai Lama dead or alive, but they were too late. He has arrived safely in India. His successor, the Panchen Lama, has agreed to co-operate with the Chinese.

The disguised Dalai Lama escapes from Tibet in the dark robes of a servant.

CUBA FREED FROM DICTATOR

REJOICING IN HAVANA

Jan 2, Havana, Cuba There has been a coup in Cuba, and President Batista has fled to the Dominican Republic. He has ruled Cuba, an island in Central America, as the cruel dictator of a police state for many years. Since he came to power the rich have become richer. Havana is full of Cadillacs, luxury houses and gambling casinos. But most Cubans are penniless and many are starving. There are few jobs, no unemployment benefits, and no health care.

The coup was led by a young lawyer, Fidel Castro. He rode into Havana yesterday on a tank. His second-in-command is an Argentinian doctor, Che Guevara. In 1956 they began their guerrilla attacks from the mountains. In 2½ years their small band of adventurers has become a national movement. There was great rejoicing all over Cuba today that Batista's rule has ended.

Fidel Castro, the leader of the coup in Cuba

CASTRO WELCOMED IN WASHINGTON

April 15, Washington Fidel Castro has been given a great welcome on his arrival for talks with the Vice-President. The United States is pleased that he will hold free elections in Cuba. Castro was sworn in as Prime Minister in February. Manuel Urrutia is the President.

THE US THINKS AGAIN

July 18, Havana The United States is now worried that Castro is going too far. He has dismissed Urrutia and made himself President of Cuba. He is dividing large sugar estates and distributing the land to Cuban farmers. Many of these estates belong to Americans. The United States has controlled Cuba's economy in the past, importing two-thirds of Cuba's sugar at fixed prices. Castro seems to be moving towards Communism. He is also executing Batista's supporters after speedy trials.

MORE TROUBLE IN VIETNAM

July 9, Saigon, South Vietnam Communists in South Vietnam have rebelled against the republican government. They are supported by the Viet Cong (forces of the Viet Minh) in North Vietnam. Today they killed two American soldiers. The South Vietnamese army is being trained by the United States.

PEACE IN SIGHT FOR CYPRUS

Dec 14, Nicosia Both Greeks and Turks in Cyprus are hoping for peace at last. The British are leaving the country. They have allowed Archbishop Makarios to return from exile, and today he has become President of a new independent Cyprus. His Vice-President is Turkish. Colonel Grivas has disbanded EOKA and left for Greece. After four years of bitter fighting both sides pray that Greeks and Turks will be able to forget their differences and live peacefully together.

KHRUSHCHEV MEETS EISENHOWER

Sept 20, Los Angeles Five days ago Mr. Khrushchev stepped out of his Russian plane, the most advanced jet the Americans had ever seen. He is visiting the United States for two weeks. In Washington he presented President Eisenhower with a model of a rocket. The real rocket had landed on the moon only a few hours earlier. The American President was a little taken aback by this reminder of the Russians' success in space!

Russian leader Nikita Khrushchev with US President Eisenhower (left), during Mr. Khrushchev's visit

KENYA'S EMERGENCY ENDS

Nov 10, Nairobi The Mau Mau rebellion is over. Hundreds of forest fighters have been captured. About 10,000 Mau Mau have been killed. They in turn killed about 2000 Kikuyu civilians, 1000 government troops, and 58 Europeans and Asians. The land question, which started the terrorist attacks, is being looked into by the government.

NEWS IN BRIEF . . .

'THE BRAIN' WAS CHEATING

Nov 2, New York Charles Van Doren will resign from his teaching job at Colombia University. This handsome and popular man has admitted that he won $129,000 dishonestly. In the TV quiz show, 'Twenty-One', he answered the hardest questions, week after week. He was as popular as a film star all over America. But one of his rivals spilt the beans. The most popular quiz competitors were shown the answers in advance. Other competitors who were shown the answers include an 11-year-old girl who won $32,000.

YOUNG PEOPLE WITH MONEY TO SPEND HELP THE ECONOMY

Nov 8, London The economy is booming. Teenagers have more money than ever before. They are buying soft drinks, fast food, clothes and records. Sales of 7-Up, Pepsi and Coke have soared. Because pop music is so popular, 70 per cent of all records are bought by teenagers. Many people in their twenties can afford the new Minis. These little cars are cheap and reliable. With more people driving, more roads have to be built. Britain's first motorway, the M1, was opened this week.

The new M1 motorway being swept ready for opening

PEOPLE OF THE FIFTIES

Sir Anthony Eden, British politician 1897–1977

Anthony Eden was born in the north of England. He was a gifted linguist, and studied Arabic and Persian. He was elected as a Conservative MP in 1923. He was Foreign Secretary when Hitler invaded Austria in 1938. He resigned because he did not agree with the way Neville Chamberlain gave in to Hitler. Later he became Foreign Secretary twice more, and Prime Minister in 1955. Eden welcomed Khrushchev to London in 1953, to try to ease the East-West tension. He helped to solve an oil dispute in Iran in 1954. He was responsible for establishing SEATO. Eden was much criticized for the warlike way in which Britain handled the Suez crisis. This led to his resignation as Prime Minister on January 9 1957. In 1961 he became the Earl of Avon.

Sir Stanley Matthews, footballer 1915-

Outside-right Stanley Matthews is said to have been the greatest dribbler of all time. Certainly he showed his great talent in the FA Cup Final of 1953. He began his career in 1931, playing for Stoke City and later Blackpool. His first international match was in 1938, and over the years he played in 53 more.

In the New Year's Honours List of 1965 he was made a Knight – the first footballer to be called 'Sir'. Shortly afterwards, at the age of 50, he gave up his footballing career.

Agatha Christie, novelist 1890-1976

Dame Agatha Christie will be remembered for a very long time because of the two characters she created: Hercule Poirot, and Miss Jane Marple. They appeared in dozens of her detective novels. Agatha Christie's play *The Mousetrap* was on stage continuously for 40 years. *Murder on the Orient Express* and *Death on the Nile* have each been filmed twice.

After her marriage to Colonel Christie ended in divorce, in 1930 she married a distinguished archaeologist, Max Mallowan. She became a Dame of the British Empire in 1971.

Jomo Kenyatta, Kenyan politician 1894-1978

His real name was Kamau wa Ngengi. He grew up in a Kikuyu village, at the time when the British started to colonize Kenya. He went to a mission school, and could speak English well. He spent two years in Moscow, and 20 years in London. He studied anthropology, and wrote a book about the Kikuyu people, *Facing Mount Kenya*.

In 1946 he returned to Kenya, and became head of the Kenya African Union. He was a very powerful speaker. He wanted Africans to have equal opportunities with whites. In 1953 the British accused him of leading Mau Mau. He was imprisoned for nine years. In 1964 he became President of an independent Kenya. He was immensely popular. Everyone called him 'Mzee' (Elder, or Old One). Under his Presidency Kenya had a free press, and good health and education services.

Eva (Evita) Perón 1919-52

Eva Perón was born in a tiny village, but grew to be the most influential person in Argentina. She was an actress before she married Juan Perón in 1945. She campaigned tirelessly for her husband, especially among the poorer people. With the money she raised, Eva Perón was able to increase workers' pay, and open hundreds of new schools and hospitals. In 1949 Eva Perón formed a feminist movement, and persuaded her husband to change the law so as to allow women to vote. She fell ill, and three years later died of cancer. The people of Argentina mourned in their thousands. They called her a saint.

Elvis Presley, American singer 1935-77

Elvis grew up in the Southern state of Mississippi. He often heard 'blues' music sung by black singers, and he imitated them. One day in 1954, a recording company wanted to engage a white singer who could sound like a black singer. Elvis was exactly what they were looking for. Two years later he released 'Heartbreak Hotel', the first of 45 recordings that sold over a million copies. Elvis changed the whole art of pop singing by his personality. After two years in the army he was back in show business, but the strain was beginning to tell. He put on weight, and took drugs. He died in the huge house he had bought in Memphis, Tennessee.

Grace Kelly (Princess Grace of Monaco) 1929-82

Grace Kelly was born in Philadelphia, USA. When her schooldays were over she studied drama, and was soon playing in films opposite well-known actors, including Gary Cooper and Clark Gable. When she played Bing Crosby's wife in *Country Girl* (1954), she received an Academy Award for best actress. The great Alfred Hitchcock chose her to be his leading lady in *Dial M for Murder* (1954), and *To Catch a Thief* (1955). He said she had the elegance and appeal he wanted.

On April 19 1956 her life changed. She married the ruler of the little state of Monaco, Prince Rainier II. They had three children. Her death was quite unexpected. She was driving with her younger daughter on a winding hilly road in the south of France. She had a stroke, and the car went out of control. It plunged down an embankment. Her daughter survived the crash.

Ernesto Guevara de la Serna (Che Guevara) 1928-67

'Che' Guevara was an Argentinian, an athlete, a scholar, and a medical doctor. But he devoted his life to fighting corrupt regimes. He felt that people in underdeveloped countries should struggle to be free of dictatorship and poverty. He met Fidel Castro in Mexico, and together they went to Cuba. They led the guerrillas against Batista's government. Che Guevara became a Cuban citizen when Castro took power, and served in his government. In the 1960s he joined Patrice Lumumba's national movement in the Congo (Central Africa). When that failed he became a guerrilla leader in Bolivia (South America). In 1967 he was captured by government forces there, and shot.

For the first time ever

1950	USA	Photocopier machines available
		Pre-recorded tapes produced
	UK	A company starts to sell air charter holidays
		Schools start 'O' and 'A' level exams
1951	W. Germany	Long-playing records on sale
	USA	Atomic energy produces electric power
		Experiments with colour TV are successful
	UK	A supermarket is opened
		Zebra crossings come into use
		Cities experiment with adventure playgrounds
1952	USA	A heart pacemaker is fitted
		Video recorders are on sale
		Painting-by-numbers kits on sale
	UK	Tea is sold in tea-bags
1953	UK	Successful open-heart operation
		The Samaritans established
	Germany	A fan heater is marketed
	USA	Music synthesizers invented
1954	USSR	An atomic power station opened
	USA	A vaccine for polio is developed
		TV dinners are advertised
	UK	First comprehensive school
		The government introduces VAT
		A supersonic fighter plane flies
1955	USA	Tranquillizers are in general use
		Transistors are used in radios
	UK	Firms issue luncheon vouchers
		A Wimpy bar is opened
		Bird's Eye package fish fingers
	France	Non-stick saucepans on sale
1956	Switzerland	A Eurovision song contest is held
	USA	Go-karts become popular
	UK	The government launches Premium Bonds
		Wall cracks can be filled with Polyfilla

1957	USA	Portable electric typewriters on sale
		Frisbies are all the rage
	UK	Microwave ovens on sale
	Japan	Transistor radios produced
1958	UK	A planetarium is opened
	USA	Windsurfing becomes popular
		Stereo records are on sale
1959	USA	Transistors used in computers
		Identikit used
	UK	A trial post-code is used
		A walk is organized for charity
		A drive-in bank opens

New words and expressions

New inventions, and new habits and occupations, cause people to invent new words. They also invent new slang. These are a few of the words and phrases used for the first time in the 1950s in England and America.

astronaut	fall-out
bathyscaphe	hippy
best-seller	leisure clothing
bikini	a mobile
brand image	neat (slang)
brinkmanship	pesticide
the buck stops here!	sputnik
cinerama	square (slang)
cool (slang)	teddy boy
to dig (somebody,	terylene
something)	video
disincentive	
egg-head	

How many of these words and expressions do we still use today? Do you know what they all mean?

Glossary

abdicate: to give up the throne

abduct: to kidnap

anthropology: the study of human beings

archaeology: the study of the past, usually by digging up objects buried in the ground

asthma: a disease which causes difficulties in breathing

asset: something or someone useful, worth having

become extinct: die out for ever

BOAC: British Overseas Airways Corporation (now part of BA)

call-up: notice to serve in the armed forces.

to campaign: to make the public interested in something, often an election

casual labour: workers who are hired for a short time; seasonal employment

coexistence: living together

compulsory: forced; something you are made to do

corrupt: acting unlawfully, often to gain money

Cypriot: a native of Cyprus

denounce: accuse, disagree with officially

depose: remove from the throne

fossil: remains of an animal or plant that has been preserved, and is still recognizable

guerrilla fighters: people who fight independently; not in the regular army

Kremlin: fortified part of a Russian town; in this case, the place in Moscow where the government sits

at loggerheads: disagreeing strongly

lottery: a raffle organized by the state to raise money

memento: something you keep in order to remember someone, or some occasion

mudflat: stretch of mud by river or sea, uncovered at low tide

nuclear scientist: someone working on atomic projects

oath: a solemn promise

orbit: the path of a satellite round a planet

pact: agreement, treaty

paratroops: soldiers who are dropped by parachute

philosopher: a person who studies knowledge, wisdom

pilgrim: a person who makes a special journey to a religious place

pseudo-: false, pretending

radioactive: atomic explosions cause 'radioactivity', or a change in the structure of a cell. If cells in a human body are affected, the person becomes permanently ill

satellite: a natural or artificial object that goes round the earth – the moon is a natural satellite

stratosphere: layer of air high above the earth

USSR/Soviet Union: these names refer to the same country

veto: forbid, reject

vaccine: a liquid used to inject people as a protection from disease. The vaccine is usually a mild form of the disease itself

Further reading

Post War World series; *USSR since 1945*: Elizabeth Campling. Batsford 1990

Portrait of a Decade series; *The 1950s*: Nance Lui Fyson. Batsford 1995

Living through History series; *Britain in the 1950s*: Monica Hodgson. Batsford 1989

Fashions of a decade: 1950s: Jacqueline Herald. Batsford 1995

The Twentieth Century: R. J. Unstead. A. & C. Black 1974

How we used to live 1954–1970: Freda Kelsall. A. & C. Black 1987

The Fifties: Neil Thomson. Franklin Watts 1993

The Forties and Fifties: Nathaniel Harris. Macdonald Educational 1985

Index